SCHIRMER'S LIBRARY
OF MUSICAL CLASSICS

Vol. 899

JOHANN SEBASTIAN BACH

Concerto
In D minor
Two Violins and Piano

Edited and Fingered by

EDUARD HERRMANN

G. SCHIRMER, Inc.

DISTRIBUTED BY
HAL•LEONARD®
CORPORATION
7777 W. BLUEMOUND RD. P.O. BOX 13819 MILWAUKEE, WI 53213

Concerto for Two Violins

J. S. Bach

* The Violins have to play the Tutti.
18900

A

B

Largo, ma non tanto

Solo

Solo

espressivo

espressivo

Largo, ma non tanto

poco piano

A

C

18900

18900

SCHIRMER'S LIBRARY
of Musical Classics

VIOLIN AND PIANO
SERIES ONE

ACCOLAY, J. B.

L. 905	Concerto No. 1, Am (Schill).

BACH, J. S.

L. 1111	Concerto, E (Herrmann).
L. 1601	Concerto, Gm (Nachèz).
L. 1401	Concerto, Am (Herrmann).
L. 1503	Sonata No. 1, Bm (Kortschak-Hughes).
L. 1507	Sonata No. 2, A (Kortschak-Hughes).
L. 1487	Sonata No. 3, E (Kortschak-Hughes).
L. 1516	Sonata No. 4, Cm (Kortschak-Hughes).
L. 1525	Sonata No. 5, Fm (Kortschak-Hughes).
L. 1533	Sonata No. 6, G (Kortschak-Hughes).

BAZZINI, A.

L. 1445	Op. 15.	Allegro de Concert (Auer).

BEETHOVEN, L. VAN

L. 468	Op. 24.	Sonata, F (Brodsky-Vogrich).
L. 467	Op. 30.	Sonata, No. 2, Cm (Brodsky-Vogrich).
L. 74	Op. 47.	Sonata, A. "Kreutzer". (Brodsky-Vogrich).
L. 234	Op. 40, 50.	2 Romances (Schradieck).
L. 233	Op. 61.	Concerto, D.
L. 232		Sonatas. Complete (Brodsky-Vogrich).

BÉRIOT, C. DE

L. 409	Op. 12.	Air Varié, A (Schradieck).
L. 410	Op. 15.	Air Varié, E (Schradieck).
L. 781	Op. 16.	Concerto No. 1, D (Schradieck).
L. 229	Op. 32.	Concerto No. 2, Bm (Schradieck).
L. 215	Op. 70.	Concerto No. 6, A (Schradieck).
L. 216	Op. 76.	Concerto No. 7, G (Schradieck).
L. 675	Op. 100.	Scène de Ballet.
L. 782	Op. 104.	Concerto No. 9, Am (Schradieck).

BRAHMS, J.

L. 1395	Op. 77.	Concerto, D (Zimbalist).
L. 1301	Op. 78.	Sonata, G (Kniesel-Bauer).
L. 1302	Op. 100.	Sonata, A (Kniesel-Bauer).
L. 1303	Op. 108.	Sonata, Dm (Kniesel-Bauer).
L. 1452		Hungarian Dances (Joachim-Auer), Bk. I.
L. 1453		The Same. Bk. II.

BRUCK, M.

L. 217	Op. 26.	Concerto, Gm (Schradieck).
L. 1398	Op. 46.	Scotch Phantasy (Zimbalist).

CHAUSSON, E.

L. 1782	Op. 25.	Poème.

CONUS, J.

L. 1635	Concerto, Em (Zimbalist).

CORELLI, A.

L. 525	La Folia. Variations (Léonard-Lichtenberg).
L. 8	Sonata, D (Cadenza by Joseph Hellmesberger) (Dessoff-Franko).
L. 9	Sonata, C (Ries-Franko).

DANCLA, C.

L. 1400	Op. 77.	3 Concert Solos (Svečenski) sp.e.
L. 785	Op. 89.	6 Airs Variés. First Series (Svečenski).
L. 1431	Op. 118.	6 Airs Variés. Second Series (Svečenski).

DAVID, F.

L. 237	Op. 16.	Andante and Scherzo Capriccioso (Schradieck).

FRANCK, C.

L. 1235	Sonata, A (Lichtenberg-Adler).

G. SCHIRMER, Inc.

DISTRIBUTED BY
HAL•LEONARD

A-1200

Violin I

SCHIRMER'S LIBRARY
OF MUSICAL CLASSICS

Vol. 899

JOHANN SEBASTIAN BACH

Concerto

In D minor

Two Violins and Piano

Edited and Fingered by

EDUARD HERRMANN

G. SCHIRMER, Inc.

DISTRIBUTED BY

HAL•LEONARD®
CORPORATION

7777 W. BLUEMOUND RD. P.O. BOX 13819 MILWAUKEE WI 53213

Concerto for Two Violins

Violin I

J. S. Bach

Violin I

Largo, ma non tanto

(The theme is to be played with a full, soft tone)

Allegro

Violin I

Violin II

SCHIRMER'S LIBRARY
OF MUSICAL CLASSICS

Vol. 899

JOHANN SEBASTIAN BACH

Concerto
In D minor
Two Violins and Piano

Edited and Fingered by
EDUARD HERRMANN

G. SCHIRMER, Inc.

DISTRIBUTED BY
HAL•LEONARD®
CORPORATION
7777 W. BLUEMOUND RD. P.O. BOX 13819 MILWAUKEE, WI 53213

Concerto for Two Violins

Violin II

Vivace

J. S. Bach

(The Tutti have to be played)
Tutti

18900

Largo, ma non tanto   Violin II

(The theme is to be played with a full, soft tone)

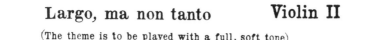

Violin II

Violin II